THE INAPPROPRIATE BABY BOOK

THE Inappropriate BABY BOOK

Jennifer Stinson

Andrews McMeel
Publishing

Kansas City • Sydney • London

THE INAPPROPRIATE BABY BOOK

Andrews McMeel Publishing, LLC
an Andrews McMeel Universal company
1130 Walnut Street, Kansas City, Missouri 64106

14 15 16 17 18 WKT 18 17 16 15 14 13

ISBN: 978-0-7407-2723-8

Book design by Holly Ogden
Illustrations by Jennifer Stinson

ATTENTION: SCHOOLS AND BUSINESSES
Andrews McMeel books are available at quantity discounts with bulk purchase for
educational, business, or sales promotional use. For information, please e-mail the
Andrews McMeel Publishing Special Sales Department: specialsales@amuniversal.com.

Dear _____,

Welcome to this magnificent world! Most traditional baby books record silly things like first haircuts and how much you weighed. They leave out all the gross and fascinating stuff that make parents laugh, scream, and scratch their heads. This book was designed to preserve those special, inappropriate moments in your life that will delight your family for the years to come. I apologize for all the embarrassment it will cause you in the future and hope you understand that it was made out of love.

Many strange things happen to a woman's body when she is pregnant! Here are some of the things that happened to your mother:

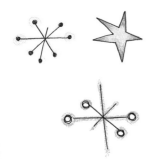
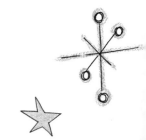

Your mother's labor experience can be described as follows:

Your parents had the following silly and/or
inappropriate nicknames for you
when you were a newborn:

Your first poop happened on this day:

And was this color:

This person changed
your first diaper:

Your belly button stump was lovingly
cleaned by this person:

Until it fell off on this day:

You were introduced to a rectal thermometer
on this day:

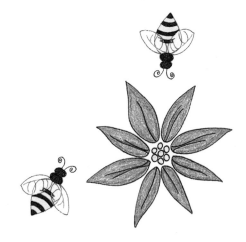

The first time you had to have mucus sucked out
of your nose with a rubber bulb was:

The first person you spit up on was:

The first person you peed on was:

Some people think it is inappropriate to breast-feed a baby in public. Here are some of the places where your mom breast-fed you:

Your mom was embarrassed by breast leakage
in the following places:

Here are some public places where you
had your diaper changed:

The first solid food you ate was:

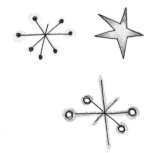

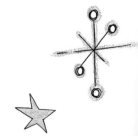

It produced an interesting poop that looked like this:

The first inappropriate thing you tried to put in your mouth was:

The first indigestible item
that came out in your diaper was:

o

o

o

o

o

o

An embarrassing outfit your parents dressed you in
looked like this:

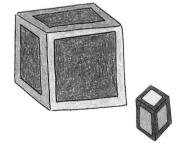

The first time you pooped or peed in the bathtub was:

When you farted in this public place, your parents were afraid people would think it was them:

Babies love to smear things. You especially
loved to smear:

Here are some public places where you were allowed to play naked:

The first item that got lodged in your nose was:

It was removed by:

Some inappropriate habits you developed were:

Your first inappropriate word was:

Like all babies, you are growing up too fast! Many parents save a baby bootie or lock of hair to remember their infant's first year. Here is something inappropriate your parents saved:

Thank you for all the wonderful memories,
and best wishes for the inappropriate years ahead.